August 1982

Dearest Mama,

I hope you enjoy looking at th[e]
as Mrs. Hurst liked dancing!

With all my love,

Mary-Jane

Mrs Hurst Dancing

And Other Scenes from Regency Life 1812–1823

Mrs Hurst Dancing

And Other Scenes from Regency Life 1812–1823

WATERCOLOURS BY DIANA SPERLING · TEXT BY GORDON MINGAY

London   Victor Gollancz Ltd   1981

Mum teaching her hopeful son a step

ISBN 0 575 03035 6

Photoset in Great Britain by Rowland Phototypesetting Ltd,
Bury St Edmunds, Suffolk
Printed in Italy by Arnoldo Mondadori Editore, Verona

PUBLISHER'S NOTE

The illustrations in *Mrs Hurst Dancing* come from two sketchbooks painted by Diana Sperling between the years 1812 and 1823. They are reproduced here exactly the same size as Diana painted them, and, as in the originals, the pictures are on the right-hand page. Captions and comments that appeared on the facing page are also included where they appeared in the original. Most of these are in Diana's own handwriting but careful observers will notice that some appear to have been amended in another hand.

The sketchbooks were given to Mr and Mrs Neville Ollerenshaw of Chichester, Sussex, by a lifelong friend, Miss Silver, a relation of the artist. Everyone who reads and enjoys *Mrs Hurst Dancing And Other Scenes from Regency Life 1812–1823* will be grateful to the Ollerenshaws for sharing their unique possession with a wider audience.

Anyone, it seems, could mess about with water-colours, and most young ladies did. But what a joy to discover another really skilful and enchanting performer. Diana Sperling's Regency sketchbook has come to stand on the shelf beside my Victorian and Edwardian favourites.

When I first began to turn over these pages I did not know which attracted me most: the innocent wit, the air of spontaneous gaiety, the stylistic charm or the insights into how these young country people lived. The spectacle of Mrs Hurst dancing, without a partner, but with an admiring audience, seems to epitomize the gay independence of rural ladies.

It particularly intrigued me that Diana's birth—gentle but only of the minor gentry—did nothing but good to her art. In those less grand country houses, with fewer servants, where she and her friends lived, the family could take an active part in the life of the estate, cleaning, decorating, planting. And things could go wrong, raising the laughs that cheer this sketchbook. The Sperling girls had to squash their own spiders on bedroom walls, carry a change of shoes in a bag when they walked out to dinner in single file behind "The Lord of the Manor", and often lose a slipper in the park mud. As for picking themselves up after yet another tumble from a horse or donkey, the humour of that hazard never seems to have palled. True, the Sperlings could boast of a real artificial

lake in their park. But when they went fishing it was from a quaint thatched hut instead of an elegantly pillared "temple".

Elegance, however, is very much a part of Diana's Regency style. Her slender, elongated figures, especially the gentlemen, have a chic all their own. Quite a contrast to the down-to-earth plumpness that pervades Queen Victoria's sketch-books. No doubt Diana has studied her botanical specimens without the loving accuracy that was to be the pride of the "Edwardian lady" a century later. Diana's fir trees look a little like bottle brushes. But her soldiers, who survived Waterloo to be sketched by her the following year, might have galloped straight out of a Jane Austen novel. Incidentally, the only other echoes of wars I heard in this country oasis came from the seasonal attack on a wasps' nest.

Perhaps the contentment that fills these pages is a function of the artist's limited existence. Her sketchbooks are not even escapist, for she seems to have been cheerfully unaware of the outside world. Her social life depended on home-made happiness and country neighbours rather than the descents of sophisticated visitors from Town. I for one am grateful to her for opening these case-ments on to a countryside "away from it all" both in time and atmosphere.

London, April 1981

TITLE PAGE ILLUSTRATION

Mum teaching her hopeful son a step

Dancing, like riding, fencing, polite conversation, a command of French, an ability to write amusing letters, and a skill at carving a joint at table ("without bespattering the company with the sauce") were some of the many accomplishments expected of the well-educated gentleman. Dancing was prized not merely as an essential social attainment but also for its training in graceful carriage and correct posture. It was for this latter advantage that Lord Chesterfield begged his son to learn from his dancing master:

> Desire him to teach you every genteel attitude that the human body can be put into; let him make you go in and out of his room frequently, and present yourself to him, as if he were by turns different persons; such as a minister, a lady, a superior, an equal, an inferior, etc. Learn to sit genteelly in different companies, to loll genteelly, and with good manners, in those companies where you are authorized to be free: and sit up respectfully where the same freedom is not allowable. . . . Take particular care that the motions of your hands and arms be easy and graceful, for the genteelness of a man consists more in them than in anything else, especially in dancing.

LIST OF ILLUSTRATIONS

The delightful sketches reproduced in this volume were made by a young English lady, Diana Sperling, mainly between the years 1816 and 1823. At this time she was living with her parents, brothers and sister Isabella at Dynes Hall, a large, indeed imposing, country house situated near Halstead in Essex. Many of the sketches depict scenes in and about this house, and also in the grounds of another residence, Tickford Park, the Buckinghamshire home of the Van Hagens, who were related to the Sperlings. The reader will agree, I think, that her sketches exert an immediate attraction, not only for their subjects but also for their freshness, their humour and sense of gaiety, the sheer *joie de vivre* which they convey. They constitute also a unique social document, bringing to us over the space of some 160 years the way of life of young country people in the early decades of the last century.

The Sperlings were important local landowners in and around the parish of Great Maplestead, which lies near the Essex-Suffolk boundary between the roads running north from Halstead to Haverhill and Sudbury. The family might be said to belong to the ranks of the substantial gentry, the sort of well-to-do squires who dominated village affairs and helped fill up the county bench of magistrates. The English squirearchy contained many thousands of families of this kind, untitled but locally prominent, and collectively possessed of a large proportion of the country's land. Their origins were very various: some were the younger sons of greater families or sprang from cadet branches of the aristocracy; some had emerged from a successful career in the law or in trade, or had risen perhaps by the profits of government contracting, supplying wartime necessities to the troops or the fleet; yet others had behind them a hazardous but fruitful career as a West Indian planter, East India Company nabob, or even as an Admiral successful in obtaining more than the usual share of prize money. With their fortune they bought or built a country house, acquired a moderate estate to go with it, and so achieved social respectability; and typically the rents of the estate were supplemented by the profits of some industrial or commercial enterprise, or by the interest yielded by holdings of government bonds, Bank of England or East India stock, or canal shares.

Like many others of these middling gentry families the Sperlings' standing as landowners was of relatively recent origin. There is some doubt about the exact date of their purchase of Dynes Hall, but it was in about 1765. Up until that time they had lived at Chigwell in the south-western corner of Essex, much nearer to London and so more convenient for their business as London fur merchants.

The Sperlings, indeed, had not very long ranked as native English, for the first of the family to settle in this country arrived only near the end of the seventeenth century. They were in fact of distinguished Swedish ancestry: the first Henry Sperling to set up in business in London was a nephew of Count Joachim Sperling, Field Marshal Royal of Sweden. George Sperling, younger brother of Count Joachim, left Sweden in 1653 to trade as a merchant in the old Hanse port of Danzig. His son Henry, who also became a merchant, moved first to Amsterdam, where he may have acted as his father's agent, and then in the autumn of 1698 decided to emigrate permanently to London. He established his business on Laurence Pountney Lane, off Cannon Street, very near the site of the Steelyard, the Hanseatic merchants' home in medieval London. He was naturalized in 1700, by a special Act of Parliament, and eventually settled in Chigwell and began to buy farms in Essex near Haverhill, not far from Halstead.

It was his son Henry, who, in partnership with his brother John in the 1730s and 1740s, developed a large and profitable enterprise which had numerous links with the Continent and the Levant. The fur trade at this time was an important branch of world commerce, and to supply the demand for pelts to make the fashionable beaver hats trappers penetrated the great forests of northern Europe as well as the wilds of North America, and merchants travelled across the Great Lakes to buy furs from the American Indians.

The rise of the Sperling family into the ranks of the Essex gentry was signified by the purchase of Dynes Hall with its estate of 500 acres and "finely wooded park". The third Henry Sperling, grandson of the first Henry who settled in England, was evidently a figure of some note in county society, serving as a magistrate and turnpike trustee, and in 1777 he was appointed High Sheriff of Essex. He was the grandfather of the artist whose pictures appear here.

Dynes Hall itself was named after the Dynes family who had resided on the spot in the thirteenth century; there may well have been a medieval hall on the site, for certainly the lordship of the manor passed into the hands of the Sperlings and so to Diana's father, John. When it was purchased by the Sperlings the house had already passed through a number of owners, having been built by William Deene, the steward—and later the husband—of the wealthy Lady Maltravers of nearby Gosfield Hall. Subsequently the property came into the possession of Mark Guyon, whose father was a successful clothier of Coggeshall, a cloth-manufacturing town only a few miles to the south of Halstead and the home of the celebrated clothier, Thomas Paycocke: his sixteenth-century house may still be seen in West Street. The elder Guyon was reputed to have acquired the enormous fortune of £100,000 from the making of the "new draperies", the bays and says—coarse woollen stuffs and worsteds—which were introduced into this part of the country from the Low Countries in the later sixteenth century. The younger Guyon, having bought Dynes Hall, reconstructed the old part of the house and built a much larger new addition, although he died in

1689 before the work was completed. It was after this time that the house came into the hands of the Bullock family, and it was from Rachel Bullock, Mark Guyon's granddaughter, that the Sperlings acquired it.

The rebuilding by Mark Guyon produced a house that displayed two quite contrasting styles: one part, the west wing, was still in the original Elizabethan design, but the main structure was Queen Anne, boasting a "seven-bay front of two storeys with three-bay pediment, parapet and hipped roof". It featured brick quoins, raised brick frames round the windows, and walls of chequered red and blue brick. A description written not long before the house came into the possession of Henry Sperling runs as follows:

> A good new house with five lower rooms 14 feet high (a hall, a withdrawing room, two parlours, one closet), a very good staircase, four chambers the same height, three large closets, four garrets with chimneys to them, very lofty, stairs up to the cupola and four good cellars. In the old building adjoining the new one, all brick, a very good hall, out of that one room more, a pantry, three chambers, one closet, over them a garret. Out of the hall a very good kitchen, four chambers over this. A good dairy, two chambers, a lower room.
>
> A new brewhouse with two or three rooms for the laundry. Three large stables, two coach-houses, four chambers over them. Two barns, one cowhouse, cart lodge and hogs-court. One courtyard. A very good garden, both enclosed with a brick wall. Good fruit and kitchen garden, two orchards and a drying yard. All the yards and gardens contain about two acres.

The Sperlings themselves carried out certain improvements, laying out drives, building new stables and forming the ornamental water in the park. At the time that Diana Sperling was making her sketches the property was owned by her father, John Sperling. Some eighty years later, about the end of the nineteenth century, it had come into the hands of an heir, Charles Brogden Sperling, DL, JP, whose son, C. F. D. Sperling, was a noted Essex antiquary in the early decades of this century. Diana, it seems, married Fred Luard Wollaston of Pimlico, and so moved away from the countryside which she recorded so attractively in her pictures. Her husband may well have been a lawyer, for he appears to have been responsible for the legal affairs and trusts of both the Sperlings and their relations the Van Hagens, of Tickford Park in Buckinghamshire. Like her sister Isabella, who married Captain George Davis of the Royal Navy, marriage came rather late, when she was about 43. We also know that in the will of John Sperling, made in 1847, she was left an annuity of a hundred pounds, the same sum as was left to her sister Isabella and her brother, the second son, Charles Robert Sperling.

We have been able to find some details of Diana's life and the family at Dynes Hall. Her mother was a widow of 31 when she married John Sperling in 1789. Harriet, the oldest of the three daughters, was born in 1790 and she married Henry Van Hagen in 1812. Diana was born in 1791 and her younger sister Isabella followed a year later. Her two brothers, Harry and Charles, were born in 1795 and 1798 respectively. At the time of the earliest sketches in this volume, about 1812 or 1813, Diana was therefore 21 or 22 years old. She died in 1862 at the age of 71.

Young ladies of her standing were carefully educated and were able to read serious books, often in several languages, and engage in intellectual conversation. They were also expected to display accomplishments such as music, fancy needlework, some knowledge of botany and natural history, and skill in drawing and painting —Diana certainly excelled at the last, and we know that she sang and had an affection for music. Young ladies of the country took great pains to cultivate their minds, as William Hazlitt remarked:

A young lady of fashion who has to devote so many hours of the day to music, so many to dancing, so many to drawing, so many to French, Italian, etc., does not pass her time in idleness . . . nor does a reviewer by profession read half the same number of productions as a modern fine lady is obliged to labour through. . . .

In the typical country house the mornings were devoted to reading, correspondence, music and sketching; in the afternoons riding and driving parties were formed of ladies and gentlemen together; and on the return home there was the interval of preparation for dinner followed by music, cards or conversation in the drawing room.

Life at Dynes Hall probably followed this pattern, though we know there were other diversions— going out to dinner, amateur theatricals, journeys to stay with friends, and visits to the poor of the parish.

Diana was probably sent to a private school for girls, perhaps the one at Great Baddow near Chelmsford, for there is a careful record in the family archives of the charges made by the two ladies who ran this establishment:

Board, needlework, English and French	£22. 0. 0.
Dancing 1 gn. entrance, & 4 gns. p.a.	4. 4. 0.
Music 1 gn. entrance, & 4 gns. p.a.	4. 4. 0.
Writing	1.12. 0.
Servants	1. 1. 0.
	£33. 1. 0.

Drawing 2 gns. p.a.
School 3 gns. entrance
Parlour boarders £25 p.a. to £30
1 Table spoon, 6 Towels, 'set of Draws'. Linen of every kind 6.

She may also have spent some time at a French finishing school at Dunkerque, near Calais, where the comprehensive charge for board, lodging, washing and dancing came to £18. 15s., with an extra guinea for French and Arithmetic, and the same addition if she took wine instead of beer with her meals. ''Tea and sugar, pens and recreation'' cost a further two guineas, while twenty lessons a month in music and drawing amounted to three guineas more. The establishment required that each lady bring with her two pairs of sheets, six napkins, a knife, fork and silver spoon (which she was allowed to take away with her when she left).

To obtain an idea of Diana herself—always "Di" in the family—we have little to go on. The sketches suggest great high spirits and an enormous sense of fun. The young Sperlings and their friends were evidently outdoor people, fond of all the activities which the extensive grounds of Dynes Hall and Tickford Park made possible—riding, hunting, coursing, walking, fishing, even swimming in the lake. Bad weather, even snow, did not deter them, nor yet the apparently considerable risk of a tumble from a horse or donkey.

Diana, it seems, could be a little sour: in one of her letters she writes that "John Sperling is going to be married to that horrid Miss Hanson—I am sure she has taken him and I fear he will repent at his leisure; at any rate it is a terrible low match." But she was also a cultured young lady who delighted in learning new songs and devoured the poetry of an earlier generation—we find her lending to her sister her copy of Beattie's *Minstrel, or the Progress of a Genius*, a long piece first published in the 1770s. She was very much a romantic. In a letter written on a visit to Southampton in February 1818 to her brother, Charles Robert Sperling, she remarks on the spell which the ruins of thirteenth-century Netley Abbey cast upon her:

It is a spot where I should like to pass *many hours* with my pencil and drawing book, Charley by my side playing his flute and a book of reflections on the encroachment of time—it is a superb ruin, but quite a ruin—on a lovely slope down to your rolling waves—which were washing the shore with a lulling and melancholy sound—you see that this beautiful ruin has inspired me with romantic ideas. . . .

Little or nothing of the workaday world creeps into the letters or the sketches. The only reminder of the recent end of the great Napoleonic struggle is when Diana painted a military review held at Dynes Hall in the year after Waterloo. The rest is all sport and amusement, or some small domestic task like papering a room or swatting flies. There is no suspicion of the turbulent events such as the collapse of the wartime prices which made farmers bankrupt and brought country banks crashing down in ruin; the unemployment and distress which followed on the release by the army and navy of their many thousands of wartime recruits; the radical agitation which led to the threatening Spa Fields assemblies and the infamous Peterloo massacre of 16th August 1819, when eleven people were killed—including a veteran of Waterloo—and four hundred were injured.

Neither is there the slightest hint of the prolonged decline of the local Essex and Suffolk cloth trades, which filled the towns with unemployed handloom weavers, and in nearby Halstead threw over two thousand of the 3,300 inhabitants on the charity of the parish. In Halstead, indeed, the bays trade was already severely in decline in 1791 when only four clothiers were still in business, and by 1800 even these four had given up while a substantial yarn-maker of the town went bankrupt.

Nor did the large-scale riots of 1816 in East Anglia create an impact: in that year when Diana Sperling was making many of her amusing little sketches armed mobs were abroad, demanding "bread or blood", incensed beyond bounds by lack of work, dear food, and the new-fangled threshing mills which were displacing the old winter standby of long hours of work in the barn with the flail. One such threshing mill had been erected at Halstead by John Vaizey, a prominent local farmer and neighbour of the Sperlings. And on 28th May a mob destroyed threshing machines and broke the windows of the principal inhabitants of Sible Hedingham, only a mile or two from Dynes Hall. Those of the rioters who were taken up by the forces of the law were lodged in the House of Correction at Halstead, where next day a great body of labourers, armed, together with large numbers of women, converged in a menacing assembly.

Very probably Diana's father, John Sperling, was much involved in these alarms and excursions. He could hardly have ignored the violent threats to life and property which appeared almost at his doorstep. But at Dynes Hall itself this tumultuous world might never have existed. The daily round of riding, entertaining, paying calls, dining out and playing cards went on as ever. One is reminded of the tranquillity of Jane Austen's characters, people not unlike the Sperlings and bound up in much the same daily routine of life. Jane Austen's first four novels, *Sense and Sensibility, Pride and Prejudice, Mansfield Park*, and *Emma*, all appeared in the war years between 1811 and 1815, but there is not a single allusion to the great European conflict, to Napoleon's blockade of this country, to Austerlitz, Trafalgar or Moscow. From her books it would never be imagined that this placid little world, absorbed in gossip, matchmaking, dowries and the trivial niceties of polite society, was a country fighting for survival.

And so it was with Diana Sperling and her sketchbooks: she concerns herself with family life and friends, with the passing of serene days in which the greatest excitement was a meeting of the hounds or the falling off a donkey. The extensive park that surrounded Dynes Hall gave privacy, as it was intended to do, but it gave more than privacy for it insulated its inhabitants from the strident and often dangerous world beyond the park gates. This, after all, was the original purpose of building a house within its own grounds, and continued to be the great attraction of a country seat. The country, as a gentleman of the period wrote, afforded

. . . simplicity and innocent contentments . . . free from city cares. The soldier's trumpet never breaks our sleep . . . no plot but upon the credulous fish, nor envy but that of birds for the prize of their song . . . Peace still slumbers by the purling fountains, peace and a secure mind which all men wish. . . .

G. E. Mingay
University of Kent
April 1981

xvi

THE PLATES

1 *Henry Van, Charles, Harry, Isabella, Di. Mrs Van—*
Pappy, Harriet V. Mum.

Dynes Hall. The family at dinner, around 1812/
1813. At the head of the table sits Diana's brother-
in-law Henry Van Hagen, who had, it seems, just
arrived as the servant is taking his coat. On the left
are her two brothers, Henry (Harry) John, the elder
of the two, and Charles Robert Sperling; then
comes her younger sister Isabella, and Diana herself. At the foot of the table, sitting on a sofa beside
a birdcage apparently containing a parrot, is Mrs
Sperling, Diana's mother. With their backs towards
us are (left to right) Mrs Van Hagen, who was
Henry's mother; Mr John Sperling, Diana's father;
and another sister Harriet Van Hagen, Henry's
wife, who appears to be feeding her dog Fairy with
titbits from the table.

Henry Van, Charles, Harry, Isabella, Di
Mrs Van- Pappy, Harriet V. Mum.

2 *Mrs Van and Harry Sperling fighting for the shuttlecock.*

This is one of Diana's earliest sketches, made in around 1812. Battledore or shuttlecocks was a children's game played especially on Shrove Tuesday, which was a day traditionally set aside as a holiday for all kinds of sports, fairs and amusements. Adults sometimes tried their hand at it, and Jane Austen mentions playing the game in one of her letters written in August 1805. The modern game of badminton was not developed until about 1870 and its beginnings were associated with Badminton House, the Gloucestershire seat of the Duke of Beaufort.

Mrs Van, & Harry Sparling fighting for the
Shuttlecock:

3 *Bathing at Dynes Hall in the old boat house.*

This is another early sketch, dating from around 1812 or 1813. The bathers are probably Harvey and Mary Grace Sperling, young relations of the Dynes Hall family. It is interesting to compare this sketch of the boat house to the one made around three years later shown in plate 17.

Sea bathing had come in during the course of the later eighteenth century, following the establishment of fashionable seaside resorts such as Scarborough, Weymouth (popularized by George III) and later Brighton, which was brought into prominence by the Prince Regent. At first such places were treated very much as the more familiar spas like Bath or Tunbridge Wells, with the typical amenities of assembly rooms, concerts and balls. The drinking of sea water for its supposed curative effects, as recommended by physicians, preceded the immersion of the body in the sea. Country gentry who had a convenient pond or lake in their grounds sometimes indulged in a dip, but there were few who—like Arthur Young at Bradfield Hall in Suffolk—made it a regular habit to be pursued throughout the year.

The children in this sketch, though, seem to be bathing purely for fun.

Bathing at D.H. in the Old boat house.

4 *Walking in the snow. Henry Van in the snow—George and Harriet, Di, Sligo and Fairy.*

Diana Sperling, with the Van Hagens' dogs Sligo and Fairy, is on the left of this sketch. The whole party are wearing the short Wellington boots which the Duke's exploits in the Peninsular War had made popular.

Walking in the snow.
Going van in the snow — George & Harriet — Di, Shop & Fanny

5   *After a well concerted plan digested on many a sleepless pillow one oversight to leave the Queen unguarded and the misery of hearing an unharmonizing tone from your adversary that there is check. Pappy and Mum.*

Diana's parents, Mr and Mrs John Sperling, playing a game of chess. Mr Sperling still wears the knee-breeches and stockings of the past century that were now going out of fashion in favour of trousers. Mrs Sperling wears the fashionable Regency style of dress covered by a pelisse or over-dress. At this time the waist was tending to become even shorter, the skirt descending from it in straight lines to just above the ankle. The bottom of the skirt was growing wider and in a few years became much more decorated, generally with rather stiff rouleaux of material. Sleeves were getting very elaborate, with exaggerated shoulders, puckered muslin being used to give the sleeves a puffed appearance.

After a well concerted plan, digested on many a sleepless pillow
one oversight to leave the Queen unguarded & the misery of hearing
an unharmonizing tone from your adversary that there is check &
Pappy & mercom.

The donkey is said to have been introduced into England in Elizabethan times: it had been widely used in the ancient world for grinding corn and driving mills to crush ores. In England also it was used for driving "gins" in mines and works, and for powering textile machinery, but its main role was in transport as a pack-bearer.

The donkeys here have been harnessed to a small carriage, and later sketches show them to have been frequently used for this purpose by the Sperling family as well as for riding. Possibly because of their size, they were considered more suitable for handling and riding by young ladies, or it may have been that at Dynes Hall only enough horses were kept for the men to ride.

Breaking in the Donkeys.

7 *A misery of human life—after an hour's perseverance, lash—obliged to give up—and return back. Harriet and Di in this predicament.*

Donkeys are notoriously obstinate and not even the combined efforts of Henry Van Hagen, Harriet and Diana could make these two cross the stream. The young people at Dynes Hall often had problems with their mounts—as later sketches show.

A Misery of human life — After an hour's perseverance
last - obliged to give up — and return back — Harriet & I, in this predicament

8 *Henry Van Hagen and Di Sperling, Dynes Hall, Essex.*

Henry Van Hagen's attempts at ploughing evidently earn the contempt of the ploughman as well as the horses. The plough in use was similar to that described by John Mortimer, the farming expert who at one time owned an estate in Essex. The implement he saw was, he said, a fine, light, wheel plough "that with two horses they plough up two acres a day"—a very good day's work by the standards of the time. This was in fact the old East Anglian plough dating from the seventeenth century or even earlier; by Mortimer's day it was fitted with an iron mouldboard "by which they make it rounding; which helps to turn the earth or turf much better than any other sort of plough". Not that Henry's efforts appear likely to do any such thing. . . .

Henry Van Hagen & Di Sperling
Dynes Hall Essex

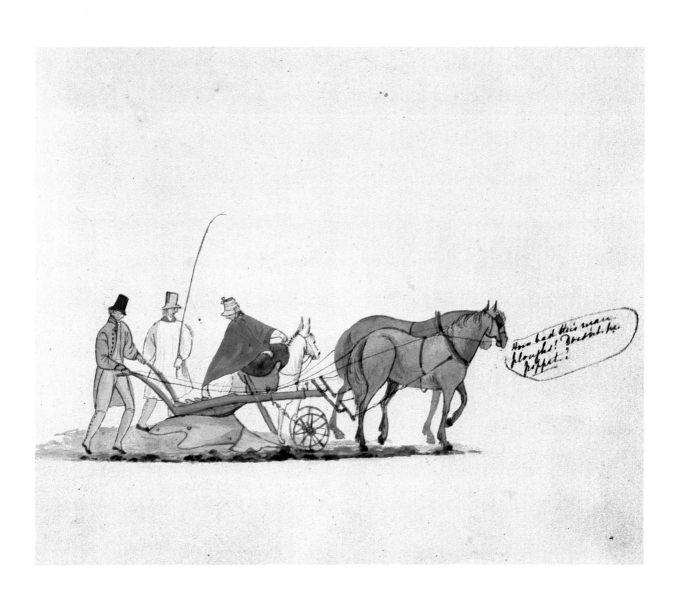

9 *A donkey race—April 8th 1816. Miss Sperling's Sprat against Mr George Sperling's Olympus.*

George Sperling belonged to another branch of the family: he was the second son of Diana's uncle the Reverend James Sperling, the vicar of Great Maplestead, the parish in which Dynes Hall is situated. George was born in 1801 and was trained as an attorney. The directories of the period show him to have been in practice in Halstead in the 1830s and 1840s, and residing at Attwoods, Halstead.

A donkey race — Miss Sperlings Sprat.
April — 8th 1816. against Mr George Sperlings
Olympire.

10 *April 16th 1816. Rolling the pitch at Dynes Hall—Essex.*

Donkeys seem to have been the jacks-of-all-trades at Dynes Hall. This one is being used to draw a heavy roller, with Diana in attendance and Henry Van Hagen apparently engaged in tracing out the border of the lawn. The exercise may have been in preparation for a game of bowls.

April 16. 1816. rolling the plat at Dynas Hall — Efsen

11 *George leaping a ditch—April 17th 1816—near Monks Lodge.*

The two sisters, Diana and Isabella, watch George Sperling's equine feat from the relative safety of their perch on their donkeys. Monks Lodge was where George's parents, the Reverend James Sperling and his wife Elizabeth, lived. It was described as "an estate and neat modern house" and was situated to the north of Great Maplestead, on the opposite side of the village from Dynes Hall.

George leaping a ditch. — April 17. 1816. near Monks Lodge —

12 *Isabella tumbles.*

Fording the ornamental water at Dynes Hall. The two unmarried sisters are on their donkeys, and the horse-riders are probably Henry Van Hagen and his wife Harriet. This is the first of many difficulties Isabella had out on riding parties.

Isabella Grimble.

13 *Playing bowls June 7th 1816, Dynes Hall. Capt Du Cane . . .*

An incident during a visit to Dynes Hall of officers of the 13th Light Dragoons for a military review. The regiment had just returned from France following the end of the hostilities which had reached their conclusion at Waterloo the previous June. An inspection of the regiment had been carried out at Romford on the 5th June 1816 by the Commander-in-Chief, who was reported as especially pleased by the beauty and condition of the horses, and the visit to Dynes Hall was part of a triumphal march which took the regiment through Chelmsford and Halstead on its way north to Bury St Edmunds and Cambridge.

Playing bowls. June 4th 1816. Dynes Hall.
Capt. Du Cane &c....

14 *The Review at Dynes Hall: June 1816.*

A colourful representation of what must have been
a memorable occasion for the family at Dynes Hall,
though it was not, it seems, too summery a day:
the ladies wear their cloaks.

The Review at Dynes Hall. June. - 1816.

15 *June 11. Cherish running off with Isabella.*

Another incident during the visit of the Dragoons officers, with Isabella mounted, unusually, on a horse—and having problems controlling it.

June 11. Cheviot running off with Isabella.

16 *Returning from a dinner party at Night. June 12th 1816.*

A last scene from the excitement of the military presence. Isabella, it seems, was again on a horse, and the three donkeys were harnessed to the open phaeton bearing the other ladies. The phaeton was a popular style of small carriage, especially designed for driving by the owner or other amateur. Here, an extra passenger is sitting on the footman's perch while the footman himself stumbles sleepily along behind the carriage.

Returning from a dinner Party at Night!
June. 12th 1816.

17 *Isabella fishing! Dynes Hall.*

The chosen place was the old boat house by the lake: a curious donkey looks on. Fishing was an unusual pastime among ladies but the girls of Dynes Hall, it seems, would try their hand at anything. At any rate, the oldest printed work published in England on the subject of fishing, from the *Book of St Albans*, 1496, is attributed to a woman, the prioress of a Hertfordshire nunnery. Isabella's rod was probably only a long twig and the line made of horse hair, taken for preference from the tail of a young stallion. She was probably hoping to catch a carp, or, perhaps, a gudgeon.

Isabella fishing!   *Dynes Hall*

18 *Harry tumbling off his colt. June 1816.*

A spot of bother, this time on the open road, as the fingerpost indicates. Harry was the elder of Diana's two brothers.

Harry tumbling off his Colt.
June. 1815.

19 *The Temple of the Waters! Dynes Hall.*

A summer scene in the beautiful woods belonging
to the Hall. Isabella and Diana seem to be gather-
ing berries or fruit, while Harriet, accompanied by
her dog Fairy, reads and Henry Van Hagen tends a
bonfire.

The Temple of the Waters. Dynes Hall

20 *Henry Van and Isabella riding on the trunk of a tree.*
July 10th 1816. Dynes Hall.

An amusing scene, complete with dog and donkeys, where the wood cutters had been at work.

Henry Pau, & Isabella riding on the trunk of a tree.
July 10th 1816. Dynevor Hall.

21 *The Table D'Hote de Bouriques! July 1816. Dynes Hall.*

"The donkeys' set meal!" It is remarkable that throughout the sketches all the figures appear fully and formally dressed, the men always wearing the customary tall hat of the period, the ladies never without their ornamented "cottage" bonnets.

Une Table D'Hote de Bourignes!

July. 1816. Dynes Hall!

22 *Charles Sperling's new invented method of conveying ladies over wet grass—Dynes Hall.*

A somewhat inclement day, one may guess, from the topcoats and cloaks. The latter were perhaps the fashionable "Wellington mantles" derived from a Spanish style made familiar by the Peninsular War. Charles Robert Sperling, the younger of Diana's two brothers, married Louise Astle, the daughter of Thomas Astle, Keeper of the Records in the Tower of London, and went to live at Stansted Mountfitchet, near Bishop's Stortford in the neighbouring county of Hertfordshire. From his correspondence we gather that he had an exceptionally large family and found himself hard pressed to live on the inheritance which his father had left him.

Charles Sperlings new invented method of
conveying ladies over wet grass — Dynes Hall.

23 *Charles Sperling picking up his sister Isabella who had rolled off her donkey—Essex.*

The accident-prone Isabella taking another fall, this time in an Essex lane where ruts, holes, mud and stones abounded.

*Charles Sperling picking up
his sister Isabella who had rolled
off her donkey. Essex —*

24 *Sheltering from a heavy shower of rain!*

Horses and donkeys rest under cover, while a plank proves too frail a support for the combined weight of the three humans.

Sheltering from a heavy shower of rain!

25 *29th August: 1816. A specimen of the Buckinghamshire roads.*

A hasty dismounting from a stranded carriage on the journey from Dynes Hall to Tickford Park, the home of the Van Hagens, in Buckinghamshire. Fairy takes an uncomfortable flight through the air while the other dog Sligo and Henry's horse add to the confusion. Harriet, Diana and Henry's mother attempt to off-load the luggage. There is no evidence to suggest that Isabella was one of the party at Tickford Park, and the woman in a plain bonnet is probably a maid.

Buckinghamshire roads, like those in Essex, evidently left much to be desired. The one shown here may well have been that from Newport Pagnell (the country town near to Tickford Park) to Bedford, described by that inveterate traveller Arthur Young as "a cursed string of hills and holes by the name of a road".

29th August: 1816.
A Specimen of the Buckinghamshire roads.

26 *Papering the saloon at Tickford Park. September 2nd 1816.*

The scene moves to Tickford Park in Buckinghamshire. This Elizabethan house, which was demolished in 1976–7, stood in what was once a deer park, and came into the possession of the Van Hagen family towards the end of the eighteenth century when the widow who had inherited it, Hannah Jaques, married Frederick Hendrick Van Hagen. He died in 1808, so that at the time Diana painted this picture the house belonged to Henry Van Hagen.

The ladies are engaged in pasting paper and fixing a border. The use of papers for decorating walls was not very old. The practice had been stimulated by the appearance of papers lighter in design and colour, produced by a process of printing from wood blocks in oil colour instead of stencilling or hand colouring. Printing of wallpapers was first developed by J. B. Jackson of Battersea in the middle of the previous century.

Papering the Saloon at Tichford Park. Sep.br 2.d 1816.

27 *The finding of the lost sheep! September 8th 1816—Tickford Park.*

The man on the right seems by his dress to have been a farm servant or park attendant.

The finding of the lost sheep! Sepr 8.th 1816.

Techford Park —

28 *Mrs Van murdering a spider. September 10th 1816. Tickford.*

An incident while the ladies were dressing in their room. There were, of course, two Mrs Van Hagens. The spider-killer was probably Henry's mother as Diana invariably referred to her sister Harriet by her Christian, rather than her married, name.

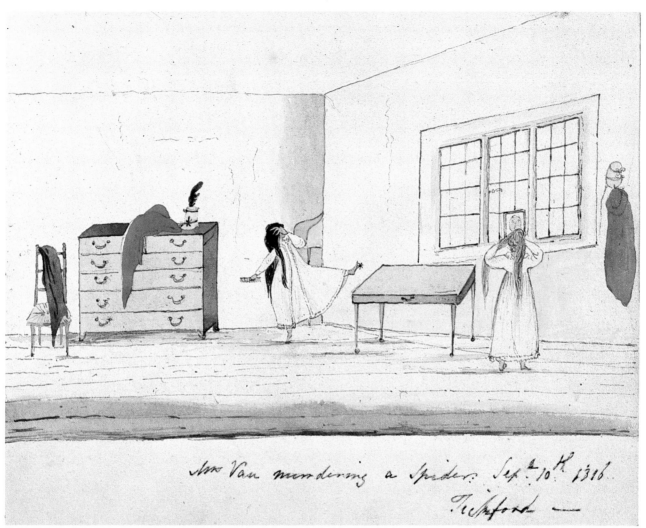

Mrs Van murdering a Spider. Sep.ᵗ 10.ᵗʰ 1316.

Teckford —

29 *The Lord of the Manor and his family going out to a dinner party at 5 o'clock with a tremendous stile before them.*

The hazards of walking to a near neighbour's for dinner. Five o'clock was a fashionable hour for dinner at this time. Luncheon had not yet assumed its later importance as a substantial meal taken in the middle of the day, and little was eaten between breakfast (usually taken about nine) and dinner. The party are carrying their house shoes or slippers. The lantern Henry carries is, no doubt, for the return journey.

The Lord of the Manor & his family
going out to a dinner Party at 5 O'Clock.
with a tremendous stile before them.

30 *A Stag Hunt in the Duke of Bedford's Park! September 1816. Buckinghamshire.*

With the growing preference for hare and fox, the stag lost pride of place in the affections of hunting men. The decline of stag-hunting in the course of the eighteenth century was reflected in the introduction of carted deer (deer imported from another area) in about 1728. Tickford Park was situated only some seven miles from the Duke of Bedford's residence at Woburn, and rather less from the limits of the Duke's park.

A Stag hunt, in the Duke of Bedfords Park!

Sep.t 1816. Buckinghamshire

31 *Carting oats off Tickford Farm.*

It looks an improbably high stack of oats for one wagon and three horses to draw to the stackyard. A curious feature of the farm-workers, both here and at Dynes Hall, is that they always affected a hat—one of them is only a little less tall than that worn by the gentlemen.

Carting oats off Pickford Farm:

32 Cricket was originally a game with plebeian associations but it became quite genteel and even aristocratic in the course of the eighteenth century. The sketch shows the old-fashioned type of two-stump wicket, the third stump not having been long introduced at this time, while the players seem also to have ignored the recent regulation concerning the size of the bat. The two-stump wicket was only a foot high with a gap of some two feet between the stumps: this space was left for the "popping" or "block" hole, into which the batsman had to put the end of his bat before the wicket-keeper could "pop" the ball into it. Bowling was fast and along the ground.

One suspects that Diana allowed herself a bit of artistic licence when she painted the refreshment table in what appears to be the middle of the pitch.

33 *Newport Pagnell. Mrs Hurst dancing. September 17th 1816.*

A record of an informal occasion, somewhat remote from the elegant balls held in high society which were well-regulated affairs, normally begun with a stately minuet. The company here may have been enjoying country dances which were extremely popular as they allowed much variety, the top couple "calling the dance" as they pleased. It was obviously an exhausting business as two of the ladies are fanning themselves after their exertions. Mrs Hurst, however, continues dancing merrily. The instrument is probably a harpsichord: this was very commonly found at this time and had not yet been supplanted by the pianoforte, which was introduced only in the later decades of the previous century.

Newport Pagnell. Mrs Hurst dancing

Sept. 17. 1816.

34 *A cottage built by the Duchess of Bedford, in the style of Henry 7th's reign. September 1816.*

This cottage is at Woburn Sands in Bedfordshire and was built in 1810–11 by Humphrey and J. Adey Repton; the motifs came from "some curious specimens of timber houses [communicated] to the Society of Antiquaries in 1810".

The "picturesque" style greatly influenced the cottages built by the owners of landed estates in the early decades of the nineteenth century. Architects like John Claudius Loudon provided owners with pattern books for the building of the cottage *"ornée"*, with all the features shown in Diana's painting: the tall ornamental chimney stack, gothic windows with little diamond panes, patterned brickwork and creeper-covered walls. The roof here is out of keeping, thatch being prescribed by the exponents of the style. Sadly, the convenience and comfort of the inhabitants were sacrificed to architectural effect.

A Cottage built by the Duchess of Bedford, in the Style of Henry 7th reign. Sep.r 1816.

35 *Sketching a cottage. September 29 1816.*

A sketching party from Tickford Park. The cottage, presumably, was the one shown on the previous page. Diana seems to have finished her painting of it in record time, and she then proceeded to paint an enchanting picture of the rest of the party as they struggled to complete their sketches.

The carriage shown here is a barouche, a design dating from the previous century and having strong royal and aristocratic associations. It was not intended for private drivers but was usually conducted by a smart professional coachman and a postillion who was seated behind on the rumble. The body, elegantly elongated, "sometimes so shallow as to be almost tray-like, was of family capacity, usually hung high on cee springs". The groom or coachman can be seen at the horses' heads: one of the horses is carrying a side-saddle, showing that one of the ladies had ridden out instead of being driven in the barouche.

Sketching a Cottage: Sep.r 29. 1816.

Although the presence of ladies on the hunting field was later made respectable by no less a personage than the Empress of Austria, women had for long featured among the followers of the hounds. It will be recalled that the Vicar of Wakefield's whole family "on some fine days rode a-hunting", and that Sophia Western damaged her nose in a fall from a horse. At this time the sport was slower and safer than it was later to become, and many huntsmen used quite run-of-the-mill untrained mounts and preferred to go round by the gate or to dismount and lead the horse over a fence rather than risk a dangerous jump. When this sketch was made the fox had not yet quite achieved its triumph over the hare, as the popularity of fox-hunting was adversely affected by the high cost of maintaining a pack of hounds and professional huntsmen, and by the scarcity of foxes—"bag foxes" were used from an early date. In a letter written in November 1819, Diana's brother Harry wrote of his hunting:

> I have changed Sappho for a mare which is a bright bay with a black mane and legs and extremely handsome. She is almost too young to hunt being only rising five but today was very near it as the foxhounds ran through this place when Reynard made into the wash house and frightened Charlotte so much she scudded off. I did not follow him as my horse wanted shoeing.

In at the death. Oct: 3d 1816. Pitchford Park

The local newspapers kept country ladies informed of the latest fashions. For example, an issue of the *Chelmsford Chronicle* of this period reported on a new style of riding habit and a "Coburg Walking Dress". The latter was described as a

> . . . round dress of fine French cambric under a pelisse of amber shot sarsnet, elegantly ornamented in a novel style of blue satin ribband. Oatlands hat to correspond with the pelisse, tied with a chequered ribband of blue on white, and the hat surmounted by a bunch of tuberoses or passion flowers. Morocco shoes or half boots of light blue, the colour of the pelisse trimming; Limerick gloves and the hair dressed forward in curls.

One lady's highly fashionable dress would require much attention to remove the grass stains before it could be worn again. . . .

Henry Van Hagen, who is courteously carrying the ladies' cloaks, is talking to a man who, from his style of dress, shorter hat, knee-breeches and stockings, would appear to be a park keeper or attendant.

Oct. 6th 1816. Slippery grass

38 *November 2nd 1816. Tickford Park—Dinner waiting at a Neighbour's house.*

Another walk to dinner, this time in November mud which must have played havoc with the ladies' fashionably flat shoes.

Nov.ʳ 2ᵈ 1816. Tichford — Dinner waiting at a Neighbours house

39 *Lion, Mrs Van Hagen's donkey tried and bought. November 3rd 1816, Tickford.*

An opportunity for trying out and buying a donkey occurs as a carrier's pack-train passes near Tickford Park. Pack-trains were still widely used at this date for carrying goods through parts of the country where the canals had not penetrated and the roads had not been improved by turnpiking. Donkeys were admirably adapted for carrying the less heavy loads: this train was probably on its way to some nearby market or fair.

Lion, Mrs Van Stagens Donkey tried & bought – Nov.r 3. 1816.
Titchfield

40 *Riding out for exercise on a dark, muddy, raining and windy day in November—The Consequences.*

Tickford Park. This is very probably a self-portrait, and it shows what a wonderful sense of humour Diana had: her horse is playing up, she has lost both her hat and comb and her hair is coming down.

Riding out for air in a dark, muddy, rainy
& windy day in Novr — the consequences

41 *Planting and digging, November 13th 1816. Tickford.*

Gardening was a favourite pursuit and had been growing in popularity since the beginning of the previous century when specialist firms of nurserymen established themselves in the western environs of London and circulated their catalogues to regular customers. At the time of this painting there was a big demand for novelties from abroad, especially for the wisteria and tea rose imported from the Far East, together with dahlias, petunias, lupins, ornamental trees like the Douglas fir from America and many others. Such was the enthusiasm that the Royal Horticultural Society was formed in 1804, and coach passengers would stop and descend in the middle of a journey in order to take a detailed view of a well-known garden on the route—one of the "rural paradises which now surround our country houses".

Henry Van Hagen's garden, judging from Diana's impression of it, seems to be a long way away from earning such a description. . . .

Planting & digging.
Novr 13. 1816. Tichford.

The whole party has returned to Dynes Hall, and probably spent the Christmas of 1816 there. One gentleman is pushing a lady around the ice on a chair while the two dogs, Brisk and Sligo, and the rest of the party look on.

Skating was a popular exercise, widely practised whenever the winter was hard enough to give a sufficiently thick covering of ice on lakes and rivers. The skates were originally made from polished bone, but ones with metal soles and blades, secured by leather straps, were in use by this time having been introduced from Holland in about 1600.

Skating on the Water at Dynes Hall

43 *With Hark and Hoop and wild Halloo! Harry coursing —Dynes Hall.*

Coursing—the use of greyhounds to pursue hares by sight rather than smell—is a very ancient sport. In Diana Sperling's day it was still more popular than the newer foxhunting, and although the law confined coursing to those who possessed the necessary qualifications of property, it was very widely followed and thousands of dogs were kept by gypsies, labourers and mendicants. "Go where you will," exclaimed Lord Torrington, "everyone is a sporter, alias poacher; every market place is overrun by greyhounds and pointers." The first coursing clubs were founded some forty years before this painting was done, the one at Swaffham, Norfolk (1776) being the first followed by the Ashdown Park in Berkshire in 1780, and the Malton, Yorkshire, in 1781. A letter written by Isabella in 1819 mentions the gift by Mr Davis of "a very good greyhound", while one of Henry's letters, written in the November of the same year, recounted how he went coursing on his horse Bluecap: "I was out an hour and a half or two hours, coursed a lease of hares and found a brace of rabbits. . . ."

Harry Coursing — Dynes Hall —

"With Hawk & Hoop & wild Halloo!" *Beau[?] courtiers*
& Wynes Hall

44 *Diana leading the donkeys thro' the mud. Fanny Hammersley inside, Mr Paris riding.*

The long dresses, pelisses and topcoats worn at this time were hardly suitable for ploughing through winter mud. The carriage is again the small open phaeton drawn by three donkeys. Fanny was a friend, as was Mr Paris: a letter written at this time by Isabella mentions that "P. has brought Diana some new songs—some are very pretty. . . ."

Mr Paris was evidently also famous for the bad manners of his chestnut horse.

Diana leading the donkeys thro' the mud. Fanny Hammersley inside Mr Paris riding.

45 *A riding party from Dynes Hall to Auberries. H. Van Hagen and Diana in front. Henry V.H. and Fanny Hammersley side by side. Mr Paris in the green coat.*

Harriet Van Hagen and Diana are the leading couple, followed by Henry Van Hagen and Fanny Hammersley. Mr Paris is relegated to the rear of the party where his bucking horse can do no damage. It is probably one of Diana's brothers on the grey horse.

Auberries was a country house a few miles distant from Dynes Hall, near to Sudbury as approached by the Halstead-Sudbury road. On the large-scale map of Essex made by John Chapman and Peter André in 1772–4, it is marked as being the residence of Robert Andrews Esquire. This gentleman and his wife were the subjects of a famous painting by Thomas Gainsborough, and the area provided many settings for Gainsborough's landscapes; the artist was born at Sudbury.

H Van Hagen & Diana in front
Henry VH & Fanny Hammersley side by side
Mr Paris in the green coat

A riding Party from Dynes Hall to Auberries:

46 *Harry in his morning dress followed by his Tailor—Dynes Hall.*

It is not clear just why the tailor was trailing after Harry Sperling—perhaps to see if a new morning dress was quite comfortable or required alteration. The local tailor or dressmaker would make visits to the country house to show the cloths and take measurements, with further visits later on for the fittings. Well-to-do people who lived as near to London as did the Sperlings, however, might prefer to order clothes direct from a London tailor who already had their measurements.

Dynes Hall.

Harry in his morning dress followed by his Tailor —

47 *Meeting the hounds returning home.*

It is noticeable that, although in the foreground, the ladies and their donkeys are drawn very small against the hounds and the horses—perhaps this was an artistic convention of the day. The hunts of this period often went out for several hours and covered great stretches of country, sometimes extending to twenty miles or more. Some hunting landlords made it a condition of their tenants' leases that they boarded out puppies on the farms and kept a couple of hounds for the hunt. Packs of hounds changed hands for £2,000 or more and it was certainly not a poor man's sport. When Sir Harry Goodricke ran the Quorn, one of the famous Leicestershire packs, it cost him as much as £6,000 a year—more than many substantial gentry families had as their total income. But cost did not deter the enthusiasts. As Lord Torrington remarked: "From our cradle there is a love of field sports handed down to us from Nimrod; and confirmed by the Norman Conquest as a right of gentry. . . ."

meeting the hounds returning home —

The gentleman on the left—possibly Mr Paris again, considering the behaviour of his chestnut horse—has lost his stirrups: the horses always seem to have been skittish when Diana's paintbox was at hand.

A ride at Auberies –

49 *Mrs Sperling murdering flies—assisted by her maid who received the dead and wounded. Dynes Hall.*

The lady of the house is engaged in the homely task of swatting flies. Diana often used a mock-military style of writing to describe everyday events.

Houses of the period were frequently plagued by mice, rats, "bugs" and flies, and professional rat-catchers and bug-destroyers would advertise their services in the newspapers. One was in attendance at Buckingham Palace, and others had many aristocratic names on their books. Many country houses had a home farm attached so that fresh produce was close at hand, but the presence of stables, dairies, pig-sties and barns in close proximity to the house was a potent source of flies in summer.

Dynes Hall.

Mrs Sperling murdering flies — assisted by her
maid who received the dead & wounded.

50 *Stephens curing a sick chicken by hunting it round the yard—Harriet and Diana looking on.*

A scene in the chicken yard. Members of the Sperling family would involve themselves in any minor happening in or around Dynes Hall. Stephens was a house or kitchen maid, and was helped here in her unsuccessful efforts to catch the invalid chicken by one of Diana's brothers, or perhaps her brother-in-law, Henry.

Even if there were no home farm, the older style of country house would still have its cowshed, pigsty and chicken house. Perishable goods could not be carried over long distances and in a severe winter country districts might be cut off from markets for weeks at a time.

Stephens curing a sick chicken by hunting it round
the yard — Harriet & Diana looking on —

51 *May 23rd. Dynes Hall. Mrs S. and Wilkinson.*

Mrs Sperling ventures out in the rain with a servant to carry her plant pots. She wears a pelisse over her dress, a garment which buttoned down the front and was sometimes cut rather short to show nine or ten inches of white muslin dress beneath. The picture reveals the existence of a billiard table in the hall. Billiards became a popular game with gentlemen in the previous century, but the cost and size of the table limited it to the well-to-do, and even in the larger houses the only place that could be found for it was in the hall. This was not always very convenient, however, and so the new houses of the nineteenth century often had a room specially set aside for the game. Frequently it was located in what eventually became the "gentlemen's suite" of the house, with a separate entrance from outside, and near the study, library, smoking room and gentlemen's cloakroom. Most country gentlemen found a billiard table to be an asset, especially when the weather forbade outside activities and male guests became restless indoors.

May 23ᵈ Dynes Hall. Mrs S. & Wilkinson

52 *May 25th. Henry Van electrifying—Mrs Van, Diana, Harry, Isabella, Mum and HGS. Dynes Hall.*

The electrifying machine is obviously Henry's latest toy. It is probably his wife Harriet looking over his shoulder, unwilling to be a party to his experiments. His mother starts the chain, followed by Diana, Harry and Isabella—who is swooning. HGS is a member of the Grace Sperling family, relations of the Dynes Hall Sperlings. Fairy is at his feet, taking no interest in the proceedings.

Experiments with electricity have a long history, although in Diana's day the phenomenon was still little more than a source of amusement. In England electricity had attracted attention as early as the sixteenth century, in the time of William Gilbert, Queen Elizabeth's physician-in-ordinary. Later on Robert Boyle noticed that false hair was easily electrified, and once carried out an experiment with the ornamental locks of "two beautiful ladies". Then in 1730 Stephen Gray performed his celebrated experiment of electrifying a boy, suspending him on threads made of hair and bringing a charged object near his feet—the current was seen to be carried along rods held in his hands. Subsequent investigators succeeded in drawing fiery sparks from a human body, and by the middle of the eighteenth century a friction machine was used for generating electric shocks to amuse the spectators at public exhibitions. Scientific curiosity continued. A Mr Boze, reported Joseph Priestley, was even so magnanimous as to say he wished to die by an electric shock "that the account of his death might furnish an article for the memoirs of the French academy of science". Parisians enjoyed seeing 180 men of the French King's Guard shocked simultaneously, and this spectacle was followed by an even more remarkable one in which a shock was passed through a mile-long line of Carthusian monks. Incautious investigators, following up the dangerous experiment of Benjamin Franklin, were killed by shocks received from the strings of kites flown during thunderstorms. Further experiments were made by Priestley and others, notably the eccentric Henry Cavendish, who was said always to dine on a leg of mutton and to speak fewer words than a Trappist monk. By the end of the eighteenth century electricity was being tried out for horticulture (the shocks did not seem to stimulate the plants) and also in medicine; it was said to be successful in relieving complaints ranging from agues, blindness and palsy to dropsy, deafness and hysteria. Many people remained sceptical, however, and when a friend of Jane Austen's asked his physician if he should try electrical treatment, she wrote: "I fancy we are all unanimous in expecting no advantage from it."

Dynes Hall.

May 25th Henry Van electrifying – Mrs Van. Diana. Harry
& Isabella – Mum & HGS

53 *Pouring out the lavender oil into the Vases, in the lavender house at Park Place: Emma, Isabella, Harvey, Diana, Elisa.*

An incident during a short visit to Park Place at Henley-on-Thames. A lavender house was a small building set aside for the preparation of lavender oil and lavender water. Lavender was used both as a perfume and as a medicine.

The making of lavender water from the oil of lavender gathered from the flowers was not uncommon among ladies of this time—though in Diana's picture the gentlemen too are lending a hand. A standard recipe ran as follows: "Half an ounce of oil of lavender, six pennyworth of ambergris, mix them together and put them to a pint and a half of the best rectified spirits of wine, shake it well two or three times a day, let it stand for two or three months, then filter it off."

Pouring out the lavender oil into the Vases, in the Lavender house at Park Place:

Emma, Isabella, Harvey, Diana, Elisa —

54 *Harry Rochfort playing his flute—D. I. and Charles.*

A romantic pastoral: Harry Rochfort sits on a rustic bench; one of the Sperling girls waters the flowers while the other relaxes on the grass beside her brother Charles.

The playing of the flute was a fairly general accomplishment among cultured young people of the leisured classes, and Diana, as we know from one of her letters, was particularly fond of it. The Rochfort family was distantly related to the Sperlings and hailed from Co. Westmeath, Ireland.

Harry Rochfort playing his flute — & I & Charles —

55 *The besieging of the Lou Chou Islands and dispersing the inhabitants by fire—This memorable event took place September 17th 1818 at YPN under the command of Carolus the bold in which they were totally routed and forced to fly for succour and for safety and their house taken away in a bucket.*

Again a mock-military style is used, this time to describe burning out a wasps' or hornets' nest. The commander of the intrepid army, Carolus the bold, was Diana's brother Charles.

The besieging the Lou Chou Islands
and dispersing the inhabitants by fire — This
memorable event took place. Sept. 17th 1818 at
9, PM under the command of Carolus the bold
in which they were totally routed & forced
to fly for succour & for safety & their
house taken away in a bucket. —

Pyper Hall   C.S.

56 *Elisa Beville fishing—September 1818. Dynes Hall—Di sitting on the round. To the left Henry Grace S. and H. Beville. Miss Bartholomew under the tree.*

Elisa Beville casts her hook (much to the danger of the onlookers) while Diana sits on the grass and a Miss Bartholomew reads under a tree. To the left is a relation, Henry Grace Sperling, and Harvey Beville.

Dynes Hall—
Di sitting on the round.
To the left Henry Grace S. & H. Beville
Miss Bartholomew under the tree

Elisa Beville fishing.   Sept. 1818

57 *Fanny and Emily Hammersley—Di Sper and Charles Sper.*

Another scene in the grounds of Dynes Hall. In the carriage drawn by a single pony are the friends of the family, Fanny and Emily Hammersley; Charles Sperling and Diana are on horseback. The tasselled rug the pony is wearing was probably for decoration, though it would also be useful for keeping off flies.

Fanny & Emily Hammersly
& Di Sper & Charles Sper

58 *Dynes Hall: Pity, a practical charade.*

Charades is a light-hearted drawing-room amuse-ment which is still with us today. In the past, charades could be very elaborate, with careful selection of appropriate costumes, stage props, rehearsals and even printed programmes.

Dynes Hall.

Pity. a practical Charade Sepr. 1818.

59   *Dynes Hall—Di and Charles.*

Diana disturbs Charles's afternoon nap—or had
he suffered a reverse in love?

60 *A walk of 11 miles—in deep mud—The pleasure of losing your way etc. The sun descending—December 7th 1818. Park Place. The spires of Reading towering before them—and the woods of PP sinking in the distance behind them.*

A winter outing during a stay at Park Place, Henley—an outing that was evidently longer than intended and with one rider too many for each mount. Park Place stands in its grounds about a mile from Henley, on the eastern side of the Thames and about six miles north-east of Reading.

A walk of 11. miles — in deep mud, — The pleasure of loseing
your way &c — The sun descending — Dec.br 7.t 1818. Park Place
The spires of Reading towering before them — & the woods of P.P. sinking in the
distance behind them

61 *Park Place: Harvey and John Sperling digging up a wasps nest at Park Place.*

Another incident on the visit to Henley: an evening foray to dig out a wasps' nest. Harvey Beville and John Sperling are hard at work.

Park Place -

Harvey & John Sperling digging up a wasps nest at Park Place

62 *Dynes Hall—Harriet and Diana riding. Mont Blanc kicking.*

A ride at Dynes Hall early in 1819. The ladies' hats have changed considerably from the simpler bonnets seen in a previous year. Both Diana and Harriet are mounted on good-looking horses (though Mont Blanc's manners leave something to be desired) and the Sperling daughters are not seen riding donkeys so often now. Even so, there was a shortage of riding horses at Dynes Hall, possibly because those few that were kept were monopolized by the menfolk. A letter of 1819 related that a proposed journey by Isabella to Gravesend to visit Charles (who was there aboard ship, waiting to sail to Napoleon's place of exile, St Helena) was deemed out of the question when the one available horse, Sappho, was found to be out of condition with bad gums and unable to eat properly. A good riding horse could cost well over a hundred pounds, a very large sum at this time.

Dynes Hall — Harriet & Diana riding —

Mont. Blanc Micking

Harry in his regimentals, trying his hand at sketching. Both he and Henry Van Hagen served in the army for a time: Henry was appointed cornet in the 16th Regiment of Light Dragoons in 1807, and Harry was made an ensign in the 9th (East Norfolk) Regiment of Foot in 1817. A cornet was the fifth commissioned officer in a cavalry regiment and carried the regimental colours; an ensign was the lowest commissioned officer of foot, who again carried the standard. Charles Sperling seems not to have served in the army, although he went out to St Helena in 1819 on a vessel carrying supplies for the establishment of the exiled Emperor Napoleon. Napoleon died there in 1821.

Harry Sperling

64 *February 1819. Priscilla Hanbury.*

A riding party from Dynes Hall watches Miss
Hanbury safely negotiate a stream.

Priscilla Hanbury

65 *Dynes Hall.*

This time it is Harry who gets a wetting. The other
members of the expedition seem unconcerned.

Dynes Hall.

It was the convention that married ladies wore caps indoors, though Harriet—now a young matron of over thirty years old—has taken to wearing one only recently. Diana and Isabella, therefore, are recognizable in this picture sitting at the table on the left, while on the right Pappy and Mum are still battling it out over the chess-board. The pictures on the walls could have been painted by Diana herself.

Dynes Hall.

67 *Mum S. at work in the minor hall—Dynes Hall—Brisk near her dozing.*

Mrs Sperling busy at some needlework; the dog Brisk keeps her company. Diana's mother died in 1854 at about the advanced age of 96—she was born in 1758. Towards the end of her life she lived with Diana and her husband, Fred Luard Wollaston, in their home at 5 Chester Place, Pimlico, London.

Mum at work in the minor hall — Dynes Hall. Brisk near her dozing —

68 *January 12th. Wilkinson feeding the pidgeons. Dynes Hall, Halstead, Essex. Mr Sperling's place.*

Winter at Dynes Hall in the January of 1820. The servant feeds the pigeons—to provide some sport with the gun at a later date?

Wilkinson feeding the pidgeons —
Dynes Hall — Halsted Essex
Mr Sperling's place

Jan.ʸ 12. Wᵐ Feeding the Pidgeons.

69 *In Lord Walgrave's Park—Essex.*

This was no doubt Lord Waldegrave's park, which lay near Borley to the north of Auberries and a few miles north-west of Sudbury. The donkeys stand by the huge stile while the ladies encourage the horse up a steep bank.

In Lord Walgrave's Park— Essex.—

70 *Langton—on the Downs—Dorset. Maynard Snow and Diana Sperling 1823.*

On the downland near Langton Lodge in Dorset in the winter of 1823. The horse appears to object to the manner in which the phaeton is being driven. Langton Lodge was the home of Mr and Mrs Snow, friends of the Sperlings.

Langton—on the Downs—Dorset

Maynard Snow & Diana Sperling

1823

POSTSCRIPT

Diana Sperling left a third sketchbook, dating from 1823 to 1833. She became much more conventional as she grew older and there is a sudden and quite profound change of style in the later book: she drew scenery, churches and other buildings instead of people, and used light washes instead of the vivid colours of the earlier paintings. She seems to have given up painting altogether after her marriage in about 1834, and no further trace of her as an artist—either under her maiden or married name—can be unearthed.